Three Reds

Anna Reckin

Three *Reds*

Shearsman Books

First published in the United Kingdom in 2011 by
Shearsman Books Ltd
Registered office: 43 Broomfield Road, 2nd Floor, Chelmsford,
Essex CM1 1SY *(please do not write to this address)*

Correspondence address:
50 Westons Hill Drive
Emersons Green
Bristol BS16 7DF

www.shearsman.com

ISBN 978-1-84861-183-2

Cover: Mary Mellor: *All the Sun Long*.

Acknowledgements
Some of these poems (some in earlier versions) have appeared in the
following magazines:

Ecopoetics, Island, Oficina de Poesia, Shearsman, Stride, The Texas Observer.

My thanks to their editors. My thanks, too, to the Faculty of Letters at the
University of Coimbra, Portugal, who, with the Municipality of Idanha-a-
Nova, offered me a residency in Monsanto in 2010: precious time to work
on old and new poems for this book.

The *Broder* series was first published as an artist's book by Traffic Street Press,
Minneapolis, in 1999 and appeared (with Paulette Myers Rich's original
illustrations) in *How2* in 2001.

Contents

Jade

Mountain Thinking

Notes on the poems

Suspend

Suspend to speak with hidden

tender as woodgrain

patience to find

the form / the tree,

make different shadows,

new light on the wall

If mirroring equals redundancy

[at best, a back-up

then I say

sides to middle, tilted
axes, the join
where silvering meets glass

Buoyed

links / skin   a stretch
             under
               dark struts

      bobs, quarrelsome, on spreading flood

           – arc against arc

joy lifts on fracture

Fruit-cage

      hand-held   reticule

         shivers of   glass

spillikin
                             seaward

    skied channels

labyrinth's a following
(maze you know or you don't)

in hedgerow's lattice
those 'negative' shapes

        – what's to catch, fall through?

trans-

    & around

        cloud formations

change in the weather:

    in darkness

        awning

Manifestation

white makes the pattern

                    via quiet lanes

etched, or as decals

              different kinds of rays and arrangements of circles

                        or dark steps in a wet field

Shoreline

in-stans, at

      rushed edge,

        want &

          fill against

   mid / met

       sand-stance

           watery connects

As if that way

Move in amongst, as if
that way
you could hear
these grave-
posts, groves of gums,
dots of tree-shade:

        stems to be lost and listening in,

        between 'here stands,' under

        stood-for's

set foot, and scatter
    stet
     – as if it could

Aquifer,

     in hydrology [dealing with the occurrence, circulation, distribution, and properties of water, of the earth and its atmosphere study of flow and force and pressure; of dreams, lakes, oceans, rivers, underground reservoirs] *rock layers that contain water and release*
[like a spray? No, more like a sponge, like pumice; but pumice comes from fire, is rock once melted, now melts stains] *and release in appreciable amounts* [flooding, rather than dripping, then; rather than erosion, drop by drop by drop]
     water-filled pore spaces, and when the pores are connected
[arcs through the rock, from space to space; would sparkle could we see it (flash floods)] *then water is able to flow through the matrix* [master (def. 18):
     in which coarse crystals or rock fragments are embedded;
         array of components and parts, as relays, tubes, transistors, naiads, magnetic storage cores, etc., for translating [
     ] one code to another. *Archaic* the womb]
       of the rock.   *may also*

18. also called **matrix**. Something to be mechanically reproduced, a mould, a container, a shaper for flow

     be called a water-bearing stratum, lens   [NL special use of *lens* a lentil, for its shape] *or zone*

Two reds,

insect-sprung, in an array of greens:

iris blades
two kinds of blood

The tension's in im-

balance,

form's inherent
movement,

each diagonal
an easeful yes

Guessed-at, hidden,
the anchor; a long way
down the sway of the line,

in another plane entirely

from this tight ship

Notes

notes

        points

lawn-spun   star

      fine-   tuning

much
      darker,

        much cooler

   mote's
        hung

      cross-hair

: tangerine

a triptych answer –

shadowy,   burn-out

stringent   harbour

dust   lime   blue

carbon-seed

broadcast

    like dust

tissue-thin redundancies

    played-out ——

        Afraid:

Pieces

Right on cue

        the magpie,

broken white

        I don't want to pick up

and the weather, of course,

so when sunshine joins the damp
I'm turning around & around
looking for indigo-violet stripes,
        a different pattern

stronger than re-assembly, the tug
and pull of resemblance

        much, much later, the rain

Framing a landscape,

or finding edges within:

dots, lines, the sway of
a wire, upsurge
of a branch

rise & fall and faster
than breathing

– the way to do it
is punctuate
in passing, compose
trees sky
hedge track
in transit,

keep finding gateways,
keep moving

earth : dirt

To know one's place

         to <u>know</u> one's place–every last blade of grass in it

    hash
    space
    pound
    well
    #   [soundless]   No:–

                fill in the blanks

We don't all speak the same language

words

discover me:
picks/stalks, as-

                  sorts of

                  shaken yarrow

                              – snapped fates
gathered,   restrewn –

net ground against net:
mechanical moiré,

swarf   precisely blurred,
an easement,
print   of spores

        this is not about light;
        not the specks that shine through.

Tracks scratched on bone, cue
heat-cracks, fault-
            lines, ask

– fingers spread –
whether, when, who: yes,
or no,

creak like roots
          search for
          water:
        the succulence of desert plants
        resin in harsh places

first, the downward strike,
then   rising,   green

            filmic,   shoot by shoot,

                    skim, scan, superimpose.

            Old lace in folds / fossils strewn / criss-cross /
            on sea-floor
        fragments] on the ledge of the café terrace
monochrome makes relief more remarkable
      — what's left
once water's driven off
           hollows, echoes, near-
                 repeats.

Let's

Let's

      the discipline of sounds   gone
      you the other side
      – half, and half again
      pennyworth of dimes

swam

                        song

List of Flowers

	rose	of Damascene
stripes	fritillary	chequerboard
snakeshead	lily	'lazy and
silly'		

she was reaching for a   narcissus

when Hades seized her

Spill

I

poppyseed:	black, (blue-black in clusters), very fine
runner beans:	glossy, pink and black, mottled, almost lustered
marigold:	green, a round cheese; dries to spiked crescents

takes the cow to market,
packed like wedges, like petals

selling the

II

crumpled poppies brave flags out of the rubble

– newborn face, fingers left in water –

unfurling
seed corn

places each bean gently, carefully spaced. Above ground a length
of twine will mark the row

III

seed leaves appear first, very plain and simple
easy to identify

IV

Lavender's blue, dilly, dilly

      – heads to the middle and inside to make bottles

     stems in and out ribbons   a spindle

Lavender's green

        seeding as perfume

           tendrils, a ladder –

V

wavering hairy stem, frail as a thread, stiffens so

        the wind can rattle it.

          Hiding in the oven

      out from under the fluted lid

      through little black windows,

VI

When I am King   a dilly bag

              scattering

    lest he be eaten

   chill kind of mettle

          You shall be Queen

Maze

There in the grocery store – chickpeas and chocolate –
she was telling me to be patient about getting lost:
to trust in the path to the centre, no matter
the setbacks, the mistakes.

But I turn aside where I am right now,
in amongst the hedges' tall green masses,
their tiny, close-set leaves,

caught by a feather,
              soft edges quivering,
              a snatch of birdsong
              two or three layers further in

      – like noticing the quick (so quick) turn of your head
            when I touch your shoulder:

                  one small arc
                              and then another

                                    – that's how it goes

Detour

One thread against another:

                intimate crossings

     Sainsbury-orange and silver birch

                  – the white bags tugging at my finger-joints

   third week of March, and we've sprung forward

      someone's turned the green man ('Walk now!')

                        upside down

Threads

Thread

Kickshaws in a twist
   – see them scramble

      carding should help: between the pins,
      all facing the same way

      then twist, and
      twist again, against
      itself
             halve the line:
        stable & ready
        against itself

Fabric

dusk	shoulders	ivies	bride's
name-tag	hips	girdle	blossom
folding	*figured*	*forced*	*repeats*
[ ]	satin	tartan	

poppets

[parition   ]

Lone Thorn

Flicker of folklore, mazy as a March weather-vane. Barbed wire,
tangles; how quickly sex smells like decay. It's that fining to a point
I have a problem with – splitting the thread, draggling the tension.
Sparks and crackles, dissipated power. Durst not gather, nor
gather round, nor deck with rags

Poor shall, poor may, poor Martha Ray

Vee-ed

Vee ---- eee ---- ed

                                –ublated

wrACKed into mAd   rags

sh: T   ShUT

                  shod-died

       thα : t   remains-s-s

'but Miss Kilman squashed the flowers all in a bunch'

miss-

1 'Her knowledge of modern history was more than respectable'

ing

2 'It was true that the family was of German origin'

so much and

3 'but her brother had been killed.'

so

4 'After all, there were people who did not think the English invariably right.'

much

BRODER

Have you ever wrote

                    posies

                              he asked:

     day's-eyed
     reflecting,
     disc edge against disc

much meaning

          in small compass?

Linen   *I*

       : spread

            –étalé

            é[toile] [a model, a pattern (in dress-making)

veil,   pinned down,

                stretched   to fit

                     mapping (pins)

on tenter-

        hooks

Linen II

        : retted, in wet fields
                        folds]
in a press, sprinkled with woodruff, wild mignonette
        –the bottom drawer–
        a little lavender   water
                        kept sweet
d[r]awn threads
stretched on the grass, in the moonlight,   to be bleached

Yokes and Hems

prick, pounce   punctuate

dotted grid
                  for gathering: fullness

                                      squeezed

feathers/fingers join

straight strips

                        herringbone / faggotting   /

                                    a gap

Openwork

:   drawn threads

    bound   lashed
                prised a-

                        part: regrouped

Separating the grasses to peer through them

:   broderie anglaise: *Instructions for eyelets:* Pierce the weave with
                                      a stiletto, then outline the hole with running
                                      stitch. Overcast the edge–closely.

    beautiful   hOles

  cunningly edged

                            lips of a scar]

Rubric

picked out in red
                    – her roughened hands
          snagged,   a repeat

sprigged, dotted
                    taut puckering
          wavers the surface
                              : reprise

Perched like a bird

       or free-arraigned

       implicit, pliée

       braid

       & its turns

hard to hem on the bias –

hangs better that way

Linho

scour, scutch, hackle, bleach, ripple, ret, beat, card, soak, dry,   break

      skin fibre pegged

   out,   dripping

            mechanical   /

                    hair

            chemical   /

                   splittings

                'within an inch of its life'

Where's the drape
in dried sticks?

I

ripo   *[for threshing]*

gyp-spaced bouquet (baby's-breath)
in the rippler's grip   :   :   :

                harvest gilt, forked
                to straw   :

                                                seeds'   : release

II

macerar   *[retting]*

dissolution rituals: ~

                [in

            still or running
                        waters;   or sometimes ~ in the fields ~
                        with dew]

                                    : ~ inside wood
                                      springs off
                                      when curled   ~

III

estender   *[spreading]*

after water, fire

                        exposed, in cones,

                                  of the sun
                         in the heat ^

IV

tascar   *[chomping]*

              forced =

                    flex   = jerked
                    in wood-
                    en jaw, snaps
                    to short straws   broken
        casings =

                    discard-

                                  ed

V

espadanar   *[scutching]*

blunt blade | | fierce brush

                              against the cork

                                        – tresses jump,

                   husks

                              a haze of motes,

                   cracked off

                                   | | sinu-
                                           ous
                                 line

VI

assedar   *[hackling]*

finer and finer

| | | | | | | | | | |

the beds of nails

| | | | | | | | | |

Unravel

Unravel

Unravel those French seams,
see if there's a selvage edge:

      zig-zag of tiny holes where the loom gripped the cloth,
      the close-pressed, ruckled warp

Ignore the little cuts of buttonholes, but caress
              the buttons,
              remove them,
              put them in a tin

Ease out each dart, each knife-edge pleat,

Unsettle sleeves, unpick pockets,
              let them open
              into nothingness

Piece by piece,

      unhook, smooth, then gently fold

Repairs

Not edge against edge

      fixed back with rivets,

      fine wires,

      pain's intimate takings

but the relief of cross-wise:

           angle & overlap

      aslant

        askance

awry   ajar

                    im-possible mends

Breakdown

as in fall: leaf-green's blazing dissolutions
as in: walls' slow cracking towards constituent stones
as in: almost every twenty-eight days, every seven years

    (*pej.*) a threat:
    to communities, communion, the (one and only) family
    as in: washing hands,
    deflecting blame
    as if unity is crystalline,
    without refractions' rainbows

    – not to hear,
    diminuendo,
    the pebble-sounds of irretrievable:
    sparrow by
    small brown sparrow,
    falling

Go there, pick up, make something new

Aubade

Be wary of the grace of aftermath. The gleam on fresh-scoured sands. Sprawled along the tideline, glyphs of wrack and mermaid's purse, starfish, embedded shells. Edge of wave as fringed lace shawl, feinting at the shore. Ladies' fingers. How discrete and pure the seagulls' cries, how high, how they make a distance. *Luxe, calme,* and hopefulness. But it's that balm I want to warn against, a daylight moon frail as the skin of milk. Minimalism's sublime – always a vasty backdrop. The relief of seeing the horizon – as if it hadn't been there all the time.

Rushes back, like the tide. What's beached here: the strong ribbed whelks with holes in their sides, or mashed till nothing's left but inmost spirals; broken glass made blunt, opaque. The opulence of salt-fed rust. Spread on a plate, the sweet scum from the top of the preserving-pan that hides the seethe below. Mistaking results for ends.

Circum-

Under lap, jug's lip

crescent moon's lost edge,

the slow sweep of a tendril –

sway, touch,   climb, bind

day or days long –

We see what horizons?

Estuary patterns: old and new channels, reticulations in sand. She
listens hard to the shell against her ear

Perfume

Soliflore I

jasmin

smoke

umbrella'd

bugle

lilas

magnolias

archways

searing

glass beads,

all in a row

Soliflore II

muguet's always
made-up: white bell

green sheath
dark moist root

> all head-space resonance, purest
> analogue

Soliflore   III
(mimosa)

Displacement makes it sweet, like unexpected music [cliché: slide
in, juxtapose] sunshine blue-grey streets down to the Harbour,
the insubstantial shade of eucalypts. Honey-sap lyric, a yellow
dust I didn't know was there.

Fougère

lavender, rosemary, geranium   *coumarin*

      a sea-calm pungency

                            eminence grise-green

      stately (breathy) flute

Chypre I

oak-moss, bergamot, rock-rose   sweet

patchouli, musk

Close harmony so tight

it squeals

hesperides   the rasp of viols

Chypre   II

[rose-madder, old rose, damascone inlay]

table-carpet, with the stove underneath; coal in the brazier.
Leaves, petals, stems compressed : exhale

close- [soft ess]
                    held   a room

Green

[floral : herbal : cut grass]

I

monocots' cream-whites
husked
with indoles

> *heavy, from southern climes*

tea-green *tilia*

> spritz, sprays, *and northern lights*

II

hedione violet
bluebell nonchalant
cool as glass

III

aromatic,
veers
to must:

> downtown showers
> old walls
> ivy dust

Still-room

as moss: grease and powdered dark

fields in jars.

iris, rose, herbs   fixture & loss

water's hungers

fleet as grass

Jade

Xing,

      I want to say

          – upwards assent –

[fire]   wood : metal : stone   [water]

        softer forms, sometimes, in harder material

hua-yi flowery-flowing,

                   and riverbeds

     grit and grind   so slow

'Don't mind going . . .'

            if, as long as –

                   hinge

Fang-gu: reproducing an ancient style

I

Hinges ¦ corners   flanged boxes

      face fits the frame, cloud shapes, dragons,

on legs   flare outwards

      – as if pushing off the line of a roof

II

peace   the stillness of a vase

    with plum blossom on it

      in season,

        real flowers, perhaps

Ancient

Bell-toll, but dips (third tone)

        valley sounds or part-way down:

                dogs barking cocks crowing, bird calls

        objects in white space / silence   (museum language)

            so precious, so heavy

wei jin yong

                so precious, so re-made

Mountain Thinking

Mons sanctus

You'd think sheer bulk 'd do it, the whole magic mass of trees

                         boulders, walls, tumbledown

barns, springs (this is hermit country), shadows, hollows and
smooth green patches that catch the sun. Slip
          slope and surface; moss, water-darkened stone

             blot out apex, arrow, acute, perforce

Especially when – instead of upwards – you swing around, anti-
clockwise, on the road that goes round the back. Nearly hidden,
among farms, the turn-off to the chapel, then a stretch of stony
waste up to the heights (monster's clamber)

– keeping on round – olives, oaks, walls, sheep-pens reappear.

Circle's done.

           Further out, across the fields, between farm buildings,

over a washing-line, peak (small mass)   quivers,   steadies,

           concentr-

                   -i-

          angul-   -ates

Surface area

It's inside

      like leaves, like trees

arbor vitae – reach, and arch, and shelter

                      [strap-like stems, a wrapping pattern]

           like breathing

        all those tiny bays, gulfs, branchings,

cells of a net, opening,   purses

               [stems and boughs use travelling stitches]

       moss transactions

    going around: the mountain's sides

                   on it, its springs –

green's [back-here

        gone there   ]

                        outwards

          like breathing

Mountain thinking

Yin is the shady side of the hill maybe needs real height for
meaning. Crags, eagles (yes, and castle-walls and look-outs
(arrow-slits)). North-facing, February mid-afternoon, and the
edge of the shadow stays just ahead of me till I've stumbled nearly
all the way down, mimosa-level, sheep-bells. Yang's been warming
my back and then when I turn he dazzles me, hides the mountain-
side with bright flashes. In the village, it's time to pick cabbages,
sit and prepare them by the back door, in the sun. Pig-smell's
sweet; daisies in pots, fruit-trees hung with wasp-trap bottles.
Here we are, the fertile plain. Base of the mountain again, the café
on the corner by the main road back; tea under a lemon tree. The
bartender scrubs the table and chair – this year's first outing. 'The
snow,' he says, swabbing them down, catching his breath. 'This
year, the snow – and the rain'. Zig-zag back up, and the kindling
I've gathered won't catch, still damp.

Miradouros

Looking out for the places I walk, but up here lanes, alleys, even the paths leading out to the countryside vanish. Plans ramble away from street-fronts, present unexpected masses. Roofs make new patterns. Little patches of garden, held up high (twenty-some terracotta flower-pots, each with its still-wintry sprig of green) obscure churches. Fountains are gone; so are the squares around them. Terraces I see, and where roofs have caved in. Granite hulks. What's private, what's wide open to the skies and the weather. Command of the heights makes serious gaps.

Menarche

I confuse with menhir: tall stones in a grey &

sombre landscape, smudges, aching

lichens, shadow   Neo-Romantic, British
                              (some foxing)
texture overlaying form,
                    blotches
                              a darkened sky

        ac
    m
  i   ter
l   ic   looks sharper than it is, a steep climb
c   up a hot and dusty road,
                     midday sun   [*a cima* here
                                          seems the
                                          usual
                                          direction

                     and down again

Can't wait to be fifty's what I thought, back then.

View

Some cities that's what you pay for. Up hill and down, all angling to get a piece of it. Screened banks.

'Just so long as you have a view,' she used to say. 'That's what matters.' But now I think a kind of sucking movement. Flying carpets window-wards and on through. Peak-hopping.

   – hope turned backward, like the angel

                              eject

                  star-burst fuselage

                                       / abject

                      to greener yonder

                                   I find I need
an edge.

Notes on the poems

pp.11, 12 and 44: 'Suspend', 'If mirroring equals' and 'Fabric' were written in response to 'Chasing Mother's Lace', a series of artworks by Joan Woods based on manipulated photographs of folded textiles.

p.18 'As if that way' is based on *Edge of the Trees*, an installation by Fiona Foley and Janet Laurence at the Museum of Sydney.

p.20 'Two reds' was written in response to *Untitled*, a relief by Mary Mellor.

p.27 'Framing a landscape' was written in response to *Sketch from a Train*, a drawing by Josey Brett.

p.34 'List of Flowers' includes material quoted from Edith Sitwell's 'Waltz' (from *Façade*).

p.39 In 'Callipygous' the quoted material beginning 'Suppose there is . . .' is from Gertrude Stein's *Tender Buttons*; 'A little sign . . . made it' is a misquote from *Tender Buttons*.

p.45 'Lone Thorn' makes reference to William Wordsworth's 'The Thorn', which tells the story of Martha Ray.

p.47 In 'But Miss Kilman squashed the flowers all in a bunch', the horizontal lines are quoted from Virginia Woolf's *Mrs Dalloway*, the vertical ones from Frances Cornford's 'Triolet'.

p.48 The introductory poem for 'Broder' includes material quoted from Rose Macaulay's *They Were Defeated*.

p.83 The phrase *weijinyong* ('for present use') in 'Ancient' comes from one of Mao Zedong's sayings concerning China's ancient heritage, *Gu wei jin yong*, usually translated as 'Let the past serve the present'.